★ ★

MINNESOTA

by Gus Gedatus

GARETH**STEVENS**
PUBLISHING
A Member of the WRC Media Family of Companies

Please visit our web site at: www.garethstevens.com
For a free color catalog describing Gareth Stevens Publishing's
list of high-quality books, call 1-800-542-2595 (USA) or
1-800-387-3178 (Canada).

Library of Congress Cataloging-in-Publication Data

Gedatus, Gustav Mark.
   Minnesota / Gus Gedatus.
      p. cm. — (Portraits of the states)
   Includes bibliographical references and index.
   ISBN-13: 978-0-8368-4669-0 (lib. bdg.)
   ISBN-10: 0-8368-4669-9 (lib. bdg.)
   ISBN-13: 978-0-8368-4688-1 (softcover)
   ISBN-10: 0-8368-4688-5 (softcover)
   1. Minnesota—Juvenile literature. I. Title. II. Series.
  F606.3.G43   2006
  977.6—dc22   2005054329

This edition first published in 2006 by
Gareth Stevens Publishing
A Weekly Reader® Company
1 Reader's Digest Road
Pleasantville, NY 10570-7000 USA

Editorial direction: Mark J. Sachner
Project manager: Jonatha A. Brown
Editor: Catherine Gardner
Art direction and design: Tammy West
Picture research: Diane Laska-Swanke
Production: Jessica Morris and Robert Kraus

Picture credits: Cover, © Bernadette Heath; pp. 4, 15, 18, 20, 22, 26, 27
© John Elk III; p. 5 © Corel; p. 6 © ArtToday; pp. 8, 10, 11 © North Wind
Picture Archives; p. 12 © Library of Congress; pp. 16, 25 Gregg Andersen;
p. 24 © James P. Rowan; p. 29 © Noah Graham/Getty Images

Printed in the United States of America

2 3 4 5 6 7 8 9 11 10 09 08 07

CONTENTS

★ ★

Words that are defined in the Glossary appear
in **bold** the first time they are used in the text.

On the Cover: The beautiful skyline of Minneapolis, one of Minnesota's
Twin Cities of Minneapolis and St. Paul.

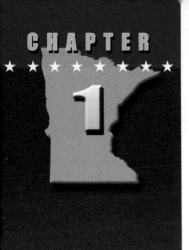

Introduction

When would you like to visit Minnesota? You can have fun at any time of year.

On New Year's Eve, fireworks light the sky over St. Anthony Falls. A few weeks later, St. Paul hosts a Winter Carnival. You can see a palace made of ice, watch people carve ice sculptures, and try a giant snow slide.

Spring and summer bring water sports and more outdoor festivals. You can attend a model boat race in Minneapolis and watch big ships dock in Duluth, too.

In the fall, Minneapolis holds a big parade. It winds through the city streets every night from Thanksgiving through December!

When would you like to visit? Whenever you come, you are sure to have a great time!

The mighty Mississippi River begins in northern Minnesota.

The state flag of Minnesota.

MINNESOTA FACTS

- Became the 32nd U.S. State: May 11, 1858
- Population (2005): 5,132,799
- Capital: St. Paul
- Biggest Cities: Minneapolis, St. Paul, Rochester, Duluth
- Size: 79,610 square miles (206,190 square kilometers)
- Nickname: The North Star State
- State Tree: Norway or red pine
- State Flower: Pink-and-white lady's slipper
- State Fish: Walleye pike
- State Bird: Common loon

History

Native Americans first came to Minnesota thousands of years ago. They hunted large animals for food and furs. They caught fish and gathered wild plants to eat, too. Later, they learned to plant crops in the rich soil.

By the 1600s, two groups of Native people lived in the area. They were the Dakota and the Ojibwa. These two groups often fought over the land. Over time, the Ojibwa took over the land in the north. The Dakota kept more to the south.

IN MINNESOTA'S HISTORY

Stone Pipes

The Dakota made fine peace pipes. They carved the pipes from stone. This "pipestone" came from quarries in southwestern Minnesota. Other tribes wanted stone pipes, too. They traded with the Dakota for the rocks. In 1937, the rock quarries were set aside by the U.S. government. The quarries now are in Pipestone National Monument.

Explorers and Settlers

People from France explored the region in the mid-1600s. The first French people to

Father Jacques Marquette explored part of Minnesota in 1673.

arrive there were fur traders. Then, in 1673, Father Jacques Marquette and Louis Jolliet reached the region. Soon after, Father Louis Hennepin arrived. He saw a big waterfall on the Mississippi River. He named it the Falls of St. Anthony.

France claimed the whole area. French traders soon built forts in the central and southern parts of this land. Some of them lived with Native people. They learned the **culture** of the Natives.

FACTS

What's in a Name?

The name of the state comes from the Dakota people. The Dakota word *minisota* means "water that reflects sky" or "sky-tinted water."

Famous People of Minnesota

William J. Mayo

Born: June 29, 1861, Le Sueur, Minnesota
Died: July 28, 1939, Rochester, Minnesota

Charles H. Mayo

Born: July 19, 1865, Rochester, Minnesota
Died: May 26, 1939, Chicago, Illinois

Charles and William Mayo grew up in Minnesota. They became doctors in the 1880s. Soon, they opened a clinic with their father. It was in Rochester. They helped many sick people at their clinic. Doctors and patients from near and far began to go to the Mayo Clinic. Now, it is one of the world's best medical centers.

In the mid-1700s, France and Britain fought over land in North America. Britain won this war in 1763. It then took over the eastern part of Minnesota. The British did not hold the area for long. Just twenty years later, the United States won the Revolutionary War. Now the United States claimed this land.

The U.S. government bought the rest of Minnesota from France in 1803. This sale was part of a big land deal. It was known as the Louisiana Purchase.

A Territory, Then a State

The U.S. Army set up forts. One of the first was Fort St. Anthony. It was built near the Falls of St. Anthony.

FUN FACTS

Where the Great River Begins

Long ago, no one knew where the Mississippi River began. Many tried to find its **source**, but they failed. In 1832, Henry Rowe Schoolcraft and a Native guide solved the mystery. They found the lake that is the start of the river. They named it Lake Itasca.

The land became part of other U.S **territories**. Few white people lived there.

The village of St. Anthony was built near a waterfall. This picture shows how it looked in 1870.

Natives held much of the land. The United States signed **treaties** with the Ojibwa in 1837. It paid them to leave their land.

More settlers began to move to the area. Some grew wheat. Others settled in what is now St. Paul. That city was founded in 1840. Later, Minneapolis grew up around St. Anthony. In 1849, the Minnesota Territory was formed. Just nine years later, Minnesota became a U.S. state. More than 172,000 people lived there by 1860.

Civil War

The new state did not allow slavery. In fact, slavery was not legal in most states in the North. Many people in the South kept slaves. They did not want to set the slaves

IN MINNESOTA'S HISTORY

The Dakota Conflict

By 1862, the Dakota had given up most of their land in Minnesota. They lived on a small **reservation**. That year, their crops were poor and the people had little food. The U.S. government had not paid them the money it owed them. The Dakota began a **revolt**. They fought the white settlers and soldiers for six weeks. Many people were killed in this fighting. In the end, the Dakota were beaten. The Dakota lost the rest of their land.

free. In 1861, the South broke away from the nation and formed a new country. It was called the Confederate States of America.

The Northern states did not want the United States to break apart. Before long, the two sides began fighting. The Civil War had begun. Minnesota was the first state to offer troops to fight for the North.

Two Vice Presidents

Hubert Humphrey was a U.S. senator from Minnesota. He was first elected in 1948. In 1964, he was elected vice president of the United States. He served in this office for four years. In the Senate, Humphrey was replaced by Walter Mondale. Mondale was elected vice president in 1976. He also served for one term. Both men ran for U.S. president and lost.

Good Times and Bad

After the Civil War, more and more people moved to Minnesota. Some cut down trees in the forests. They made lumber from the wood. Others mined iron **ore**. People in the southern part of the state grew wheat. Others found jobs grinding the wheat into flour for bread. Minneapolis became one

The war went on for four years. The North won in 1865. Then, the states came back together and slavery ended.

In the 1860s, many men worked as loggers. They used two-man saws to cut big trees into logs.

of the world's leading cities for making flour.

New railroads carried goods from Minnesota to other states. They also brought more people to live in the state.

In the 1930s, the whole nation faced hard times. These years were called the Great Depression. Many people lost their jobs, their savings, and their homes. People could not afford to buy wheat and wood from Minnesota. Many people

By the late 1800s, railroads linked Minnesota to the East and West coasts of the United States. Trains carried grain, lumber, and people back and forth. The railroads helped Minnesota grow.

in the state became poor. They suffered for more than ten years.

World War II and Beyond

From 1941 until 1945, the United States fought in World War II. Thousands of soldiers from Minnesota joined the fight. The state helped in other ways, too.

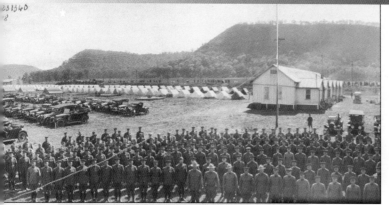

The people of Minnesota have helped the United States fight many wars. This photo, which was taken in 1918, shows Minnesota soldiers ready for action during World War I.

Miners took huge amounts of iron ore from the earth. Factories made the iron into parts for airplanes, ships, and guns. The mines and factories provided jobs to people who had been out of work for a long time.

After the war, more people moved to the state. Over time, farming became less important. More workers took jobs in factories. Some of these factories caused pollution. The waste from farms and mines also polluted the air, water, and land.

Minnesota Today

The people of Minnesota worked hard to cut back pollution. Now, the air, water, and land are cleaner.

The people of Minnesota also have passed laws to make their schools better. They are proud of what they have done, and they look forward to the future.

IN MINNESOTA'S HISTORY

Flood Damage

Floods can be a problem near Minnesota's rivers. The Mississippi flooded in 1993. It damaged much of the farmland in the eastern part of the state. The Red River of the North flooded in 1997. It damaged land in the west.

1659	The French begin to explore the region that is now Minnesota.
1673	Marquette and Jolliet follow the Mississippi River into Minnesota.
1803	The Louisiana Purchase brings all of Minnesota into the United States.
1832	Henry Schoolcraft and a Native guide find the source of the Mississippi River.
1849	The Minnesota Territory is created.
1850s	Wheat becomes a major crop in Minnesota.
1858	Minnesota becomes the thirty-second U.S. state on May 11.
1861	Minnesota is the first state to send troops to fight for the North in the Civil War.
1948	For the first time, Minnesota factories produce more goods than its farms.
1987	The Minnesota Twins win the World Series. The team wins again in 1991.
1990	The Minnesota Supreme Court becomes the first state supreme court to have more female than male justices.
1991	A record-breaking snowstorm drops 24 inches (61 centimeters) of snow in twenty-four hours.
1999	The U.S. Supreme Court says the Ojibwa may hunt, fish, and gather wild rice by their own rules rather than by the rules of the state.

People

More than five million people live in Minnesota. Most of them live in cities or large towns. Just a bit less than one-third of the people live in the country.

Minneapolis and St. Paul are known as the Twin Cities. The two cities are very close to each other. Minneapolis is on the west side of the Mississippi River. St. Paul is on the east side. More than half of the people in the state live in the Twin Cities or the nearby smaller cities and towns.

Hispanics: In the 2000 U.S. Census, 2.9 percent of the people living in the state of Minnesota called themselves Latino or Hispanic. Most of them or their relatives came from places where Spanish is spoken. They may come from different racial backgrounds.

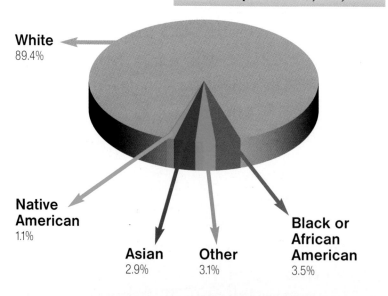

The People of Minnesota

Total Population 5,100,958

White 89.4%

Native American 1.1%

Asian 2.9%

Other 3.1%

Black or African American 3.5%

Percentages are based on the 2000 Census.

14

The People of the Past

At one time, many Native Americans lived in the area of Minnesota. White people moved onto their land and forced most of them to leave the state in the 1800s.

Most of the early white settlers came from New York and New England. Others were from Europe. In the 1800s, many people moved to the area from Germany. Others came from Sweden and Norway. In the late

St. Paul rises along the banks of the Mississippi River. This picture was taken from the Minneapolis side of the river. Together, the two cities are known as the Twin Cities.

1900s, **immigrants** came from Mexico, Southeast Asia, Asia, and Russia.

Newcomers

One large group of recent immigrants is the Hmong people. They are from Laos. They were treated badly there. Beginning in 1975,

15

More than twelve thousand students attend Minnesota State University in Mankato.

thousands of the Hmong people left their homes in Laos. Many of them made new homes in Minnesota. Today, the Twin Cities are home to more Hmong people than any other city in the United States.

Today, people still move to Minnesota from other U.S. states. Fewer people come from other countries. Only about 5 percent of the people who live in the state today were born in another part of the world. These immigrants often bring some of the culture of their home country to Minnesota.

Education

The people of this state have long believed in a good education. Since Minnesota became a state, it has had free public schools. Today, it has a strong public school system. About nine out of ten adults here have finished high school.

In 1851, the University of Minnesota opened. Now, this big university includes forty-four colleges. Eight cities are home to state colleges. The state also has more than seventy-five other colleges or universities.

Religion

Almost 90 percent of the people in the state are Christian. Of these people, most are Lutheran or Roman Catholic. Jews, Buddhists, Hindus, and Muslims also live here.

Famous People of Minnesota

Roy Wilkins

Born: August 30, 1901, St. Louis, Missouri
Died: September 8, 1981, New York, New York

Roy Wilkins was an African American. He grew up in St. Paul and went to the University of Minnesota. As a young man, he joined the **Civil Rights Movement**. He wanted to help black people get the same rights as whites. In 1955, he became head of the National Association for the Advancement of Colored People (NAACP). He helped plan the March on Washington in 1963. This march was a huge success. More than two hundred thousand people marched to show their support for equal rights. Over time, laws were changed. Thanks in part to Roy Wilkins, African Americans now have the same rights as whites.

The Land

Thousands of years ago, large sheets of ice called glaciers covered Minnesota. In some places, the ice dug into the earth. Later, when the ice melted, lakes formed. In some places, the melting ice dropped large piles of sand and rock. These piles became hills. The glaciers created much of the natural beauty of the state's land.

Lakes and Rivers

Minnesota is often called "The Land of 10,000 Lakes." In fact, it has more than 20,000 lakes! Lake Superior is the largest lake. It forms part of the state's northeastern border. The state also has about 6,500 rivers and streams. The Mississippi is the longest river in the state.

FUN FACTS

Way up North!

Minnesota is a northern state. In fact, it contains the northernmost point in all of the "lower forty-eight" states. This point is called Angle Inlet. It is home to about 150 people.

Split Rock Lighthouse perches atop a high cliff on the shore of Lake Superior.

MINNESOTA

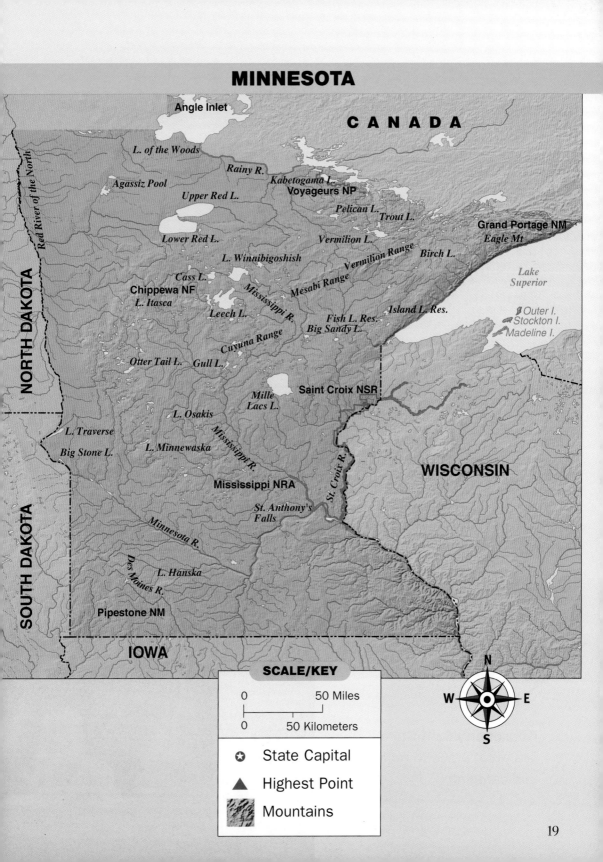

Angle Inlet

C A N A D A

L. of the Woods

Rainy R.

Red River of the North

Agassiz Pool

Upper Red L.

Kabetogama L.
Voyageurs NP

Pelican L.

Trout L.

Grand Portage NM
Eagle Mt

Lower Red L.

Vermilion L.

Birch L.

L. Winnibigoshish

Vermilion Range

*Lake
Superior*

Cass L.

Mesabi Range

Chippewa NF
L. Itasca

Mississippi R.

Outer I.
Stockton I.
Madeline I.

Leech L.

Fish L. Res.
Big Sandy L.

Island L. Res.

NORTH DAKOTA

Cuyuna Range

Otter Tail L.   Gull L.

Mille
Lacs L.

Saint Croix NSR

L. Osakis

Mississippi R.

SOUTH DAKOTA

L. Traverse

Big Stone L.

L. Minnewaska

WISCONSIN

Mississippi NRA

St. Croix R.

St. Anthony's
Falls

Minnesota R.

L. Hanska

Des Moines R.

Pipestone NM

IOWA

SCALE/KEY

0   50 Miles

0   50 Kilometers

N
W   E
S

⊛ State Capital

▲ Highest Point

▨ Mountains

A Varied Landscape

Different parts of the state have different kinds of land. In the northeast, the land is rocky and hilly. Many of the ridges contain iron ore. The state's highest point, Eagle Mountain, is in this area. It rises 2,301 feet (701 meters) above sea level.

Most of the rest of the state has flat or rolling **plains**. In the northwest, some the land is low and marshy. **Peat bogs** can be found in this area.

The southeast is the only part of the state that was not shaped by glaciers. This region is marked by rugged, rocky cliffs and deep valleys.

Major Rivers

Mississippi River
2,357 miles (3,792 km)

Red River of the North
355 miles (571 km)

Minnesota River
332 miles (534 km)

Plants and Animals

About one-third of the land in the state is forest. Many years of logging felled the older trees. The forests of the north and east now have younger spruce, birch, and fir trees. Hickory and oak are common in the south-east. Pine trees grow in the

Gooseberry Falls State Park is a great place to go hiking and camping.

center of the state. The red pine is the state tree.

Prairie grasses covered the southern, western, and northwestern parts of the state at one time. Today, most of this land is used for farming. Prairie grasses can still be seen in areas that have not been farmed.

Many wild animals make their homes in Minnesota. Deer are found all over the state. Black bear, fox, **lynx**, moose, wolves, and many small animals live in the forests and grasslands.

The state also has timber wolves. Early settlers were afraid of these animals. For many years, the state paid hunters for wolf **pelts**. By the 1970s, most wolves were gone. Laws were passed to protect the wolves. Today, more than 1,600 timber wolves live in the state.

FUN FACTS

Plenty of Parks

In Minnesota, people can enjoy nature in the cities as well as in the country. Minneapolis has 170 parks. Some are near the city's twenty-two lakes. This city has more park space per person than any other big city in the country.

The lakes and rivers are home to many kinds of fish. Walleye pike, trout, and bass are common.

Climate

Minnesota is known for its long, cold winters. The northern part of the state is especially cold. In January, the temperature there is often around 2°Fahrenheit (-17°Celsius)! The southern part of the state is slightly warmer. Summers are mild all over the state.

Economy

Many of Minnesota's early settlers were farmers. Today, the state still has many farms. Wheat, soybeans, and corn are the top crops. Dairy farming is important in the state, too.

Some settlers mined iron ore in the northeastern part of the state. Today, the richest ore is gone, and fewer people work in mining.

Early settlers also cut down trees for lumber. For many years, **loggers** felled too many trees and damaged the forests. Today, the state works to keep its forests healthy. Wood from the forests is now used to make paper and **waferboard**.

In Duluth Harbor, grain is stored in huge grain elevators and then loaded onto ships.

Factories, Banks, and More

In the past sixty years, many factories have been built in Minnesota. Some make computers and other machines. Others make simpler products, such as tape and food.

Some companies sell goods to businesses and people. About one-fourth of all workers have jobs in these companies. Other people work in service jobs. Service workers help other people. Still other people work in banking. The state has a number of large banks.

Big rivers and lakes have long been an important way to move people and goods in Minnesota. Duluth is now the largest freshwater port in the world.

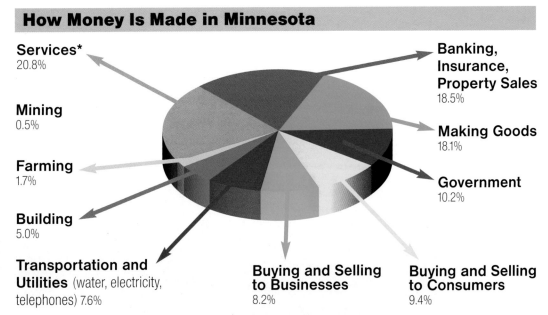

How Money Is Made in Minnesota

Services* 20.8%

Banking, Insurance, Property Sales 18.5%

Mining 0.5%

Making Goods 18.1%

Farming 1.7%

Government 10.2%

Building 5.0%

Transportation and Utilities (water, electricity, telephones) 7.6%

Buying and Selling to Businesses 8.2%

Buying and Selling to Consumers 9.4%

* Services include jobs in hotels, restaurants, auto repair, medicine, teaching, and entertainment.

Government

St. Paul is the capital of Minnesota. The leaders of the state work there. The state government has three parts. They are the executive, legislative, and judicial branches.

Executive Branch

The executive branch carries out the state's laws. The governor leads this branch. A lieutenant governor helps. The governor picks other people to work in this branch. They make up the cabinet.

The state capitol was built in 1904. Its dome is one of the largest in the United States.

Legislative Branch

The legislative branch makes laws for the state. This branch has two parts. They are the Senate and the House of Representatives.

This is the governor's mansion. It has eight bathrooms and nine fireplaces! The mansion is open to the public for tours.

Judicial Branch

Judges and courts make up the judicial branch. They may decide whether people who have been accused of committing crimes are guilty. The highest court in the state is the Supreme Court.

Local Government

Minnesota is divided into eighty-seven counties. A group of five people leads each county. The state also has about 850 cities. A mayor and a **city council** run most of them.

MINNESOTA'S STATE GOVERNMENT

Executive		Legislative		Judicial	
Office	**Length of Term**	**Body**	**Length of Term**	**Court**	**Length of Term**
Governor	4 years	Senate (67 members)	4 years*	Supreme (7 justices)	6 years
Lieutenant Governor	4 years	House of Representatives (134 members)	2 years	Appeals (16 judges)	6 years

*Senators elected in years ending in "0" serve two-year terms.

CHAPTER

★ ★ ★ ★ ★ ★ ★ ★ ★

7

Things to See and Do

In this state, people know how to have a good time! In the summer, they head to the lakes and rivers. There, they fish, swim, windsurf, and water-ski. Many people go boating. They can sail, canoe, and kayak. In fact, there is one boat for every six people in the state. This is more boats per person than any other state!

Winter is the time to cross-country ski. Some people ice skate on the frozen lakes. Others like to snowmobile. The state has more than 17,500 miles (28,164 km) of trails for snowmobiles.

Blue Mounds State Park is home to buffalo, cactus, and lots of other wildlife.

26

Enjoying Animals

This state has many hiking trails. Hikers often spot birds and other animals. Minnesota has many zoos and animal parks, too. They are home to creatures from all over the world.

Music, Plays, and Museums

The Guthrie Theater and the Children's Theater Company are two famous theaters in Minneapolis. People of all ages enjoy their plays. During the summer in some cities, plays are held outdoors. Music halls and festivals offer all kinds of concerts.

The state has many fine museums. In the Twin Cities, art museums are filled with paintings and sculpture. History museums show art, clothing,

Protected Places

If you like to fish, Voyageurs National Park is the place to go! The park has thirty lakes and lots of great fishing. Moose, wolves, and eagles also live in the park. This is just one of four beautiful areas in the state that are protected by the U.S. government.

Old steam engines are on display at the Depot Museum in Duluth. At this museum, you can even climb aboard the engines and explore!

Famous People of Minnesota

Ann Bancroft

Born: September 29, 1955, St. Paul, Minnesota

Ann Bancroft has always loved to explore the outdoors. As a child, she liked family trips in the wilderness. In 1986, she joined a group that set out for the North Pole. She finished the whole trip and became the first woman to reach the North Pole on foot and by sled. A few years later, she led three other women on a ski trip across Antarctica to the South Pole. She has earned a place in the National Women's Hall of Fame.

and other items used by the Native people and the early settlers.

The Science Museum of Minnesota, as well as the Minnesota Children's Museum have hands-on displays for young people. The Twin Cities Model Railroad Museum has model trains that move through tiny cities. All of these museums are in St. Paul.

Sports

Minnesota has four big-league sports teams. The Twins play baseball. They won the World Series in 1987 and 1991. Sports fans watch the Vikings play football and the Timberwolves play basketball. All of these teams play in Minneapolis. The state's newest pro team is the Wild. It began playing hockey in St. Paul in 2000.

Famous People of Minnesota

Prince

Born: June 7, 1958, Minneapolis, Minnesota

As a young boy, Prince Roger Nelson was good at music. He played drums, guitar, and keyboard. He signed his first record deal in 1978. He was only 19 years old. Now, Prince is a famous musician. He has had five number one hits, including "When Doves Cry" and "Cream."

Mega-Mall!

This state has the largest indoor shopping mall in the country. It is called the Mall of America. It opened in Bloomington in 1992. Bloomington is near the Twin Cities. The mall has more than 520 stores. A big amusement park and the state's largest aquarium are in the mall, too.

The Minnesota Wild is the state's pro hockey team. Here, a Wild player battles for the puck against the Los Angeles Kings in 2005.

GLOSSARY

★ ★

city council — a group of people elected to the government of a city to make decisions for the city

Civil Rights Movement — the fight for equal rights for African Americans that took place in the 1950s and 1960s

culture — the way of life for a certain country or group of people, including its history and customs

immigrants — people who leave one country to live in another country

loggers — people whose job is to cut down trees

lynx — a wildcat with a short tail, light brown or orange fur, and tufts of hair on its ears

ore — a rock that contains metal

peat bogs — areas of wet, soggy ground filled with a mossy material called peat

pelts — animal skins with the fur still on them

plains — flat lands

reservation — an area of land set aside by the government for a special purpose, such as land set aside for use by a group of Native Americans

revolt — a fight against the government

source — the start

territories — areas that belong to a country

treaties — written agreements between two or more nations

waferboard — a product made from thin sheets of wood glued together

Books

Minnesota. Rookie Read-About Geography (series). Sean Dolan (Children's Press)

Minnesota. This Land Is Your Land (series). Ann Heinrichs (Compass Point Books)

Minnesota Government Projects: 30 Cool Activities, Crafts, Experiments & More for Kids to Do to Learn About Your State. Minnesota Experience (series). Carole Marsh (Gallopade International)

The Mississippi River. Rivers of North America (series). Jen Green (Gareth Stevens)

V Is for Viking: A Minnesota Alphabet. Discover America State by State (series). Kathy-jo Wargin (Sleeping Bear Press)

Web Sites

Minnesota Historical Society Time Pieces
events.mnhs.org/Timepieces/Index.cfm

Minnesota Legislature Links for Youth
www.leg.state.mn.us/LEG/youth/index.asp

Minnesota Pollution Control Agency Kid's Page
www.pca.state.mn.us/kids/index.html

Minnesota Zoo Kids' Discovery Zone
www.mnzoo.com/education/kids_corner.asp